V&A Pattern
Pop Patterns

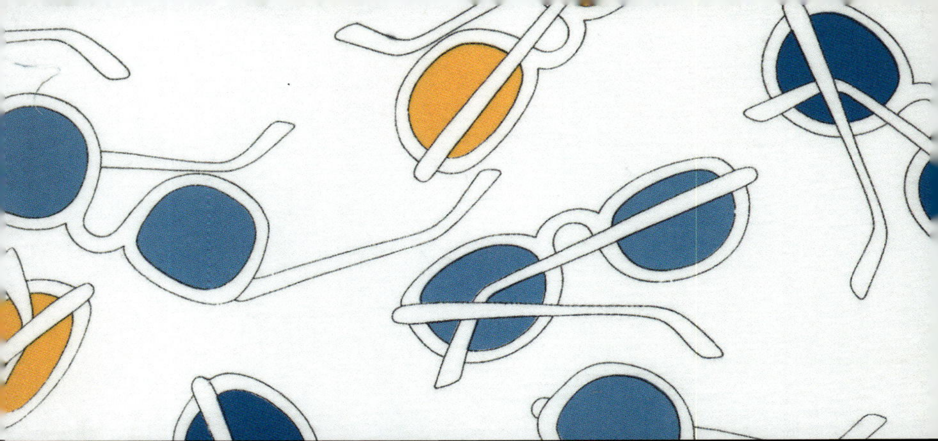

V&A Publishing

V&A Pattern

Pop Patterns

First published by V&A Publishing, 2011
V&A Publishing
Victoria and Albert Museum
South Kensington
London SW7 2RL

Distributed in North America by Harry N. Abrams, Inc., New York

ISBN 978 1 85177 636 8
Library of Congress Control Number 2010937391

10 9 8 7 6 5 4 3 2 1
2015 2014 2013 2012 2011

A catalogue record for this book is available
from the British Library.

Series Art Direction: Rose
Design: TurnbullGrey www.turnbullgrey.co.uk

Front cover (A):
Jane Wealleans/OK Textiles Ltd
Raspberry Lips, furnishing fabric. Screen-printed satin. UK, 1973 (V&A: Circ.172–1973)
Pages 2–3 (B):
Manifattura Garavaglia
Occhiali, dress fabric. Printed cotton. Italy, 1973 (V&A: Circ.512–1974)
Page 6 (C):
Screen-printed fabric on tinsel ground. UK, 1970s (T.47–2001)
Page 11 (D):
J & M Dove/Wonder Workshop
Strawberry, dress fabric. Screen-printed satin. UK, 1972 (V&A: Circ.1–1974)
Pages 78–9 (E):
Zandra Rhodes
Lipsticks, dress fabric. Screen-printed silk crêpe. UK, 1968 (V&A: Circ.266–1974)

Letters (in brackets) refer to the file name of the images on the accompanying disc.

Printed in China

V&A Publishing
Victoria and Albert Museum
South Kensington
London SW7 2RL
www.vandabooks.com

V&A Pattern

Each *V&A Pattern* book is an introduction to the Victoria and Albert Museum's extraordinarily diverse collection. The museum has more than three million designs for textiles, decorations, wallpapers and prints; some well-known, others less so. This series explores pattern-making in all its forms, across the world and through the centuries. The books are intended to be both beautiful and useful – showing patterns to enjoy in their own right and as inspiration for new design.

V&A Pattern presents the greatest names and styles in design, while also highlighting the work of anonymous draughtsmen and designers, often working unacknowledged in workshops, studios and factories, and responsible for designs of aesthetic originality and technical virtuosity. Many of the most interesting and imaginative designs are seen too rarely. *V&A Pattern* gathers details from our best objects and hidden treasures from pattern books, swatch books, company archives, design records and catalogues to form a fascinating introduction to the variety and beauty of pattern at the V&A.

The compact disc at the back of each book invites you to appreciate the ingenuity of the designs, and the endless possibilities for their application. To use the images professionally, you need permission from V&A Images, as the V&A controls – on behalf of others – the rights held in its books and CD-Roms. *V&A Pattern* can only ever be a tiny selection of the designs available at www.vandaimages.com. We see requests to use images as an opportunity to help us to develop and improve our licensing programme – and for us to let you know about images you may not have found elsewhere.

Pop Patterns
Oriole Cullen

The patterns and prints featured in this collection date from the 1960s and early 1970s, when experimentation and creativity in pattern design flourished. A new generation of designers took inspiration from 'Pop Art' – an abbreviation of popular art, the new artistic movement whose proponents questioned the accepted parameters of fine art – to create arresting, often irreverent textile and wallpaper patterns.

Pop Art had its genesis in the post-war boom in consumerism and expendability, fuelled by the advertising industry's employment of new visual tools. No longer limited to billboards and newspapers, adverts were channelled into homes and workplaces through the profusion of print media, television and film. Young British artists including Eduardo Paolozzi and Richard Hamilton parodied the industry's images, language, signs and symbols in their work, often creating collages out of newsprint and advertisements. By the early 1960s, their American contemporaries Jasper Johns, Roy Lichtenstein and Andy Warhol, among others, were creating art inspired by comic strips, celebrities, advertising and signage. In a complete departure from the dramatic, formidable art of Abstract Expressionism, Pop artists transformed the mundane and familiar, experimenting with scale, repetition and reproduction to produce striking works of art accessible to all.

The graphic two-dimensional quality of Pop Art made it an ideal source material for translation from canvas to textile prints. Experimentation with scale, unorthodox subject matter and the flat, bright rendering of colours, offered unending possibilities for textile design. Graphic depictions of everyday objects, such as household products, cigarette packets (pl.19), sunglasses (pp.2–3) and lipsticks (pp.78–9), provided instantly recognizable pattern motifs. The typography of famous brands, as found on food and drink labels (pls 12–16), was appropriated to create of-the-moment patterns in an ironic statement on the proliferation of built-in obsolescence.

As with the novelty prints popular in the 1930s–40s, Pop textiles were aimed primarily at a young market who wanted fashion-led items. In 1965 a *Life* magazine fashion feature noted: 'In this exuberant year of crazy haircuts, above knee skirts and giddy stockings, the fashion designers in search of something even farther out have turned to Pop Art.' The simple shift-like shapes popular for dresses in the period, and the flat surfaces of the t-shirt, offered the perfect media for pattern display.

The demand for Pop-inspired patterns saw well-established interior furnishing companies, such as Sanderson and Heal's in the UK, producing Pop collections. Unlike clothing fabrics, the relative permanence of furnishing textiles and wallpaper items led designers towards more abstract motifs. Neon lighting (pls 31–2) or the curved face of a juke box (pl.7) could inspire a pattern that was familiar but in some way transformed.

New technological developments had revolutionized textile production with non-woven fabrics and synthetics, but major corporations knew that surface design was just as integral to the success of their products as the properties of their fabrics and the finish of their furniture. Companies such as Courtaulds, Textra and Heal's looked to young graduate designers to produce fresh designs. Tom Worthington, director of Heal's, a London-based furniture and interior design company, recognized the need to collaborate with young designers and, as Heal's did not have an in-house design department, he employed designers on a freelance basis to pull together a collection each season from a diverse range of portfolios.

In the early 1970s, V&A textile curator Michael Regan began to assemble a collection of textiles and fashions that showed the direct influence of Pop Art in their design. The items acquired from Britain and the USA formed the basis of the exhibition *The Fabric of Pop* held at the museum in 1974. In the guide to the exhibition Regan summed up the reasons for the success and appeal of Pop prints:

> Pop Art's influence on textile and fashion design owed all its inspiration and much of its success to our mass-produced urban culture. It found its full expression in the commercialism it poked fun at and came full circle by ending up in the pages of those glossy magazines that had originally provided Pop Art with much of its imagery.

1
The Fool
Clouds, dress fabric. Printed synthetic jersey. UK, 1966–70 (V&A: T.57–2008)

2
Zandra Rhodes
Mr Man, dress fabric. Screen-printed silk crêpe. UK, 1968 (V&A: Circ.267–1974)

3
Claude Lovat Fraser, Liberty & Co.
Cactus, dress fabric. Printed silk chiffon. UK, 1973 (V&A: Circ.352C–1974)

4
Maggie Walker/Heal's
Treasure Chest, furnishing fabric. Printed cotton. UK, 1974 (V&A: T.540:3–1999)

5
Zandra Rhodes/Sanderson-Rigg Ltd
Zandra, wallpaper. Screen-printed paper. UK, 1968 (V&A: E.5088–1968)

6
Manifattura Garavaglia
Gitanes, dress fabric. Printed cotton. Italy, 1973 (V&A: Circ.513–1974)

7
Peter Jones/Arthur Sanderson & Sons Ltd
Sikhara, wallpaper. Screen-printed paper. UK, 1971 (V&A: E.229–1977)

8
In Fabrics Ltd
Jukebox. furnishing fabric. Roller-printed cotton. USA, 1973 (V&A: Circ.302–1974)

9
VIP Fabrics Inc.
Wacky Packages, furnishing fabric. Screen-printed cotton. USA, 1974 (V&A: Circ.377–1974)

10
Lloyd Johnson/Patrick Lloyd Ltd
Soup Can, dress fabric. Screen-printed silk. UK, 1973 (V&A: Circ.302–1973)

11
Jim O'Connor/Mr Freedom
Man's shirt. Printed cotton satin. UK, 1971 (V&A: T.208–1974)

12
Martini & Rossi
Martini, furnishing fabric. Screen-printed cotton. France, 1973 (V&A: Circ.367–1974)

13
VIP Fabrics Inc.
Jell-O, dress fabric. Screen-printed cotton. USA, 1974 (V&A: Circ.376–1974)

14
Anheuser–Busch Inc.
Budweiser Beer, furnishing fabric. Roller-printed cotton. USA, 1972 (V&A: Circ.192–1974)

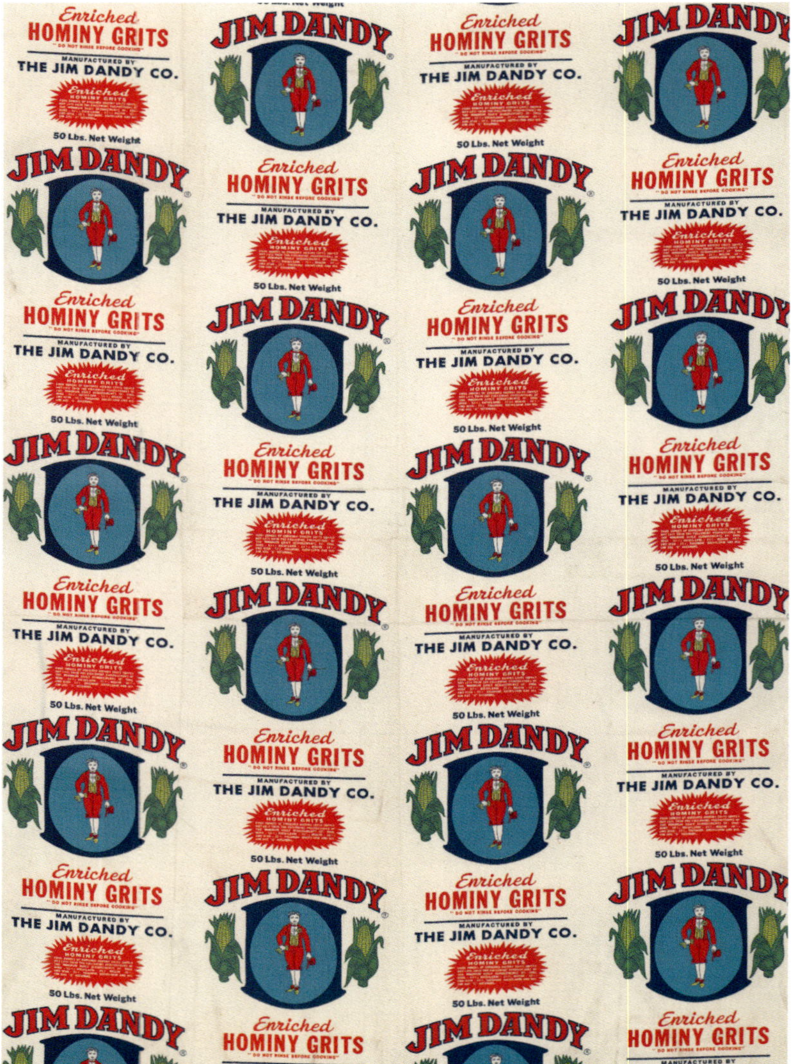

15
Avondale Mills Inc.
Grit Bags, furnishing fabric. Roller-printed cotton. USA, 1971 (V&A: Circ.20–1972)

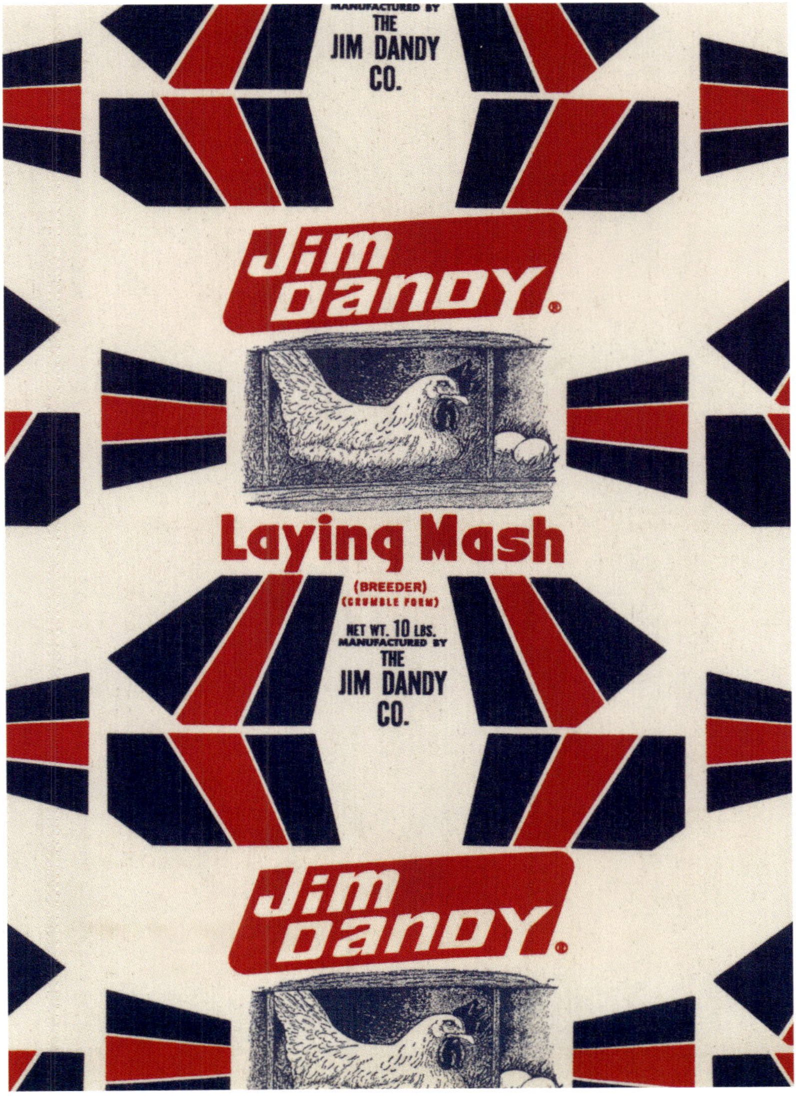

16
Avondale Mills Inc.
Laying Mash, furnishing fabric. Roller-printed cotton. USA, 1971 (V&A: Circ.19–1972)

17
Jane Wealleans/OK Textiles Ltd
Cake, furnishing fabric. Screen-printed satin. UK, 1973 (V&A: Circ.171–1973)

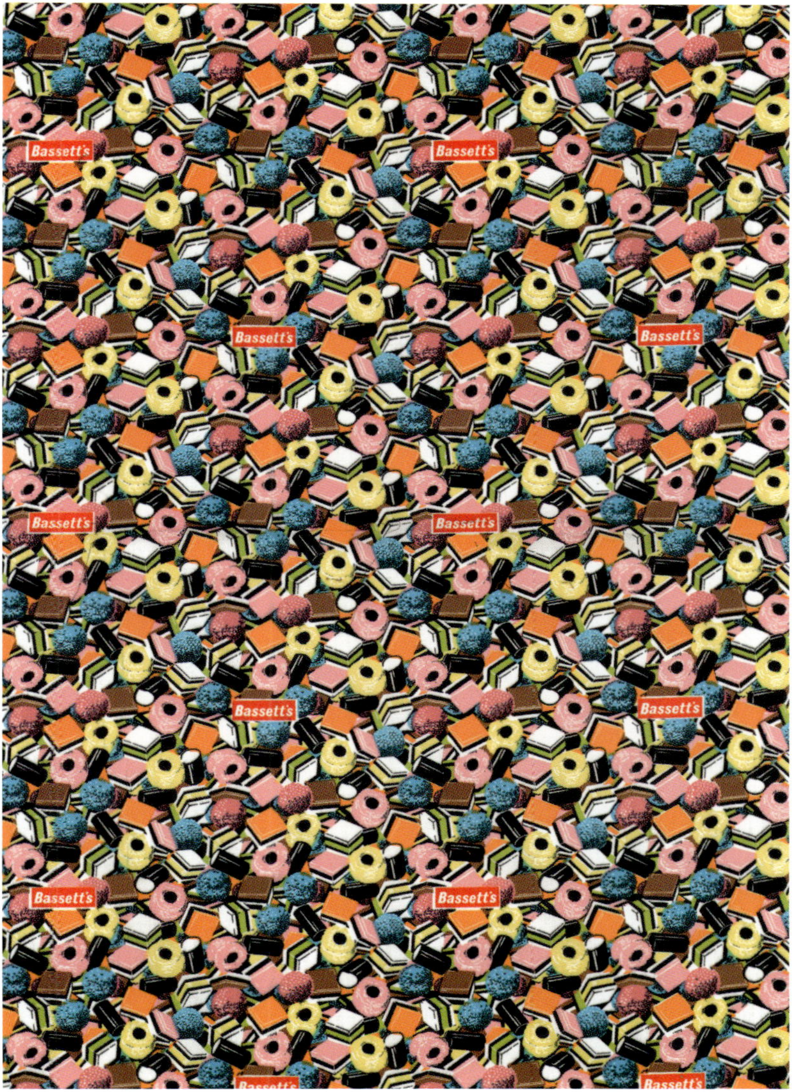

18
Geo. Basset & Co. Ltd
Liquorice Allsorts, furnishing fabric. Roller-printed cotton. UK, *c.*1932/1970 (V&A: Circ.191–1974)

19
Miss Mouse/Squeekers Ltd
Matchboxes, dress. Roller-printed cotton. UK, 1974 (V&A: Circ.442–1974)

20
Miss Mouse/Squeekers Ltd
Paints and Palettes, dress fabric. Roller-printed satin. UK, 1974 (V&A: Circ.489–1974)

21
John Wilkinson/Arthur Sanderson & Sons Ltd
Main Street, wallpaper. Screen-printed paper. UK, 1971 (V&A: E.161–1977)

22
Miss Mouse/Squeekers Ltd
Camp Coffee, man's shirt. Roller-printed cotton. UK, 1974 (V&A: Circ.488–1974)

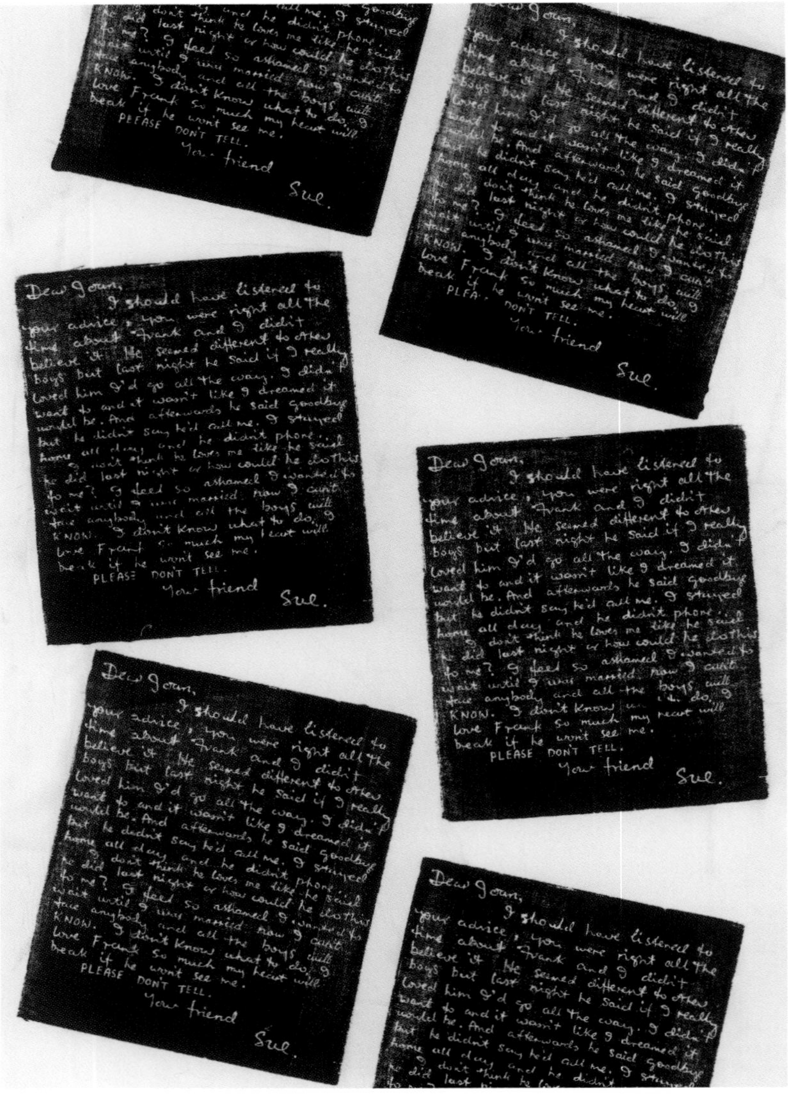

23
Lizzy Carr/Regal Robes
Dear Joan, dress fabric. Screen-printed cotton jersey. UK, 1974 (V&A: Circ.460–1974)

24
Tommy Roberts/Mr Freedom
Return to Sender, dress fabric. Screen-printed cotton jersey. UK, 1970 (V&A: Circ.236–1974)

25
Annikki & Ilmari Tapiovaara/Heal's
2&3, furnishing fabric (see also plate 26). Printed cotton. UK, 1960s (V&A: T.494:4–1999)

26
Annikki & Ilmari Tapiovaara/Heal's
2&3, furnishing fabric (see also plate 25). Printed cotton. UK, 1960s (V&A: T.494:1–1999)

27
Jane Wealleans/OK Textiles Ltd
Apples, furnishing fabric. Printed satin. UK, 1973 (V&A: Circ.170–1973)

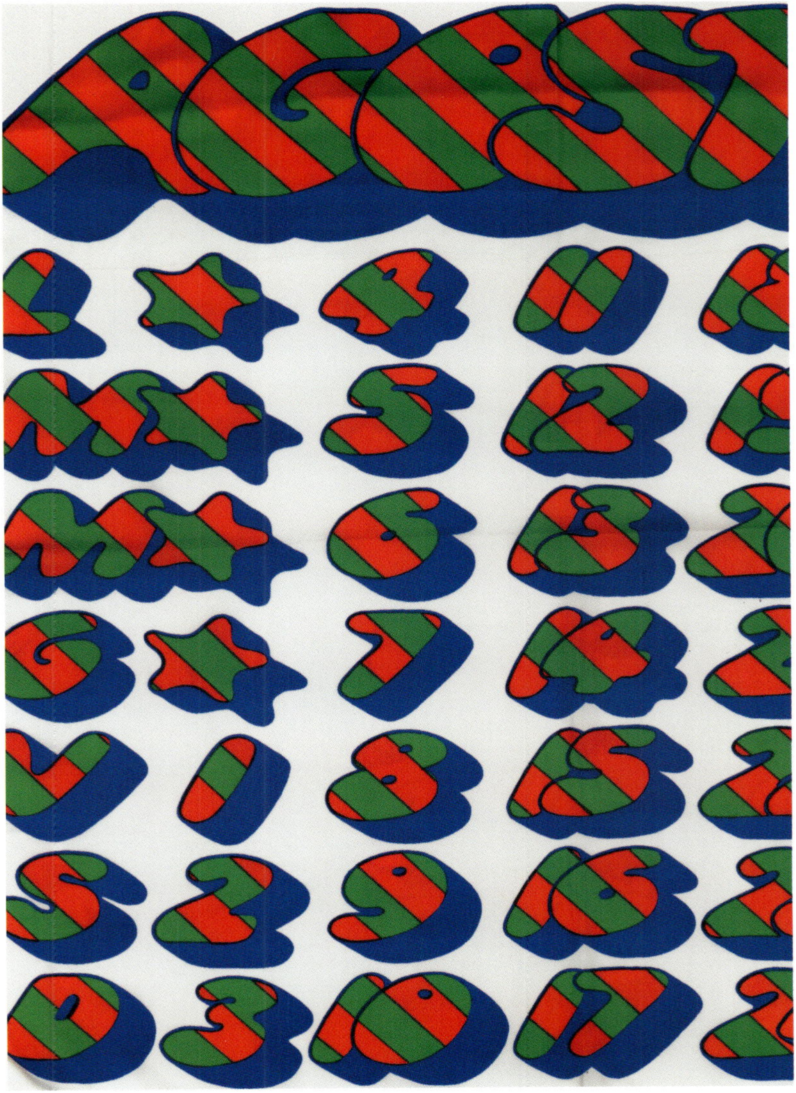

28
Crosby Fletcher Forbes/Olivetti
Head scarf. Printed silk. Italy, 1960–70 (V&A: T.223–1986)

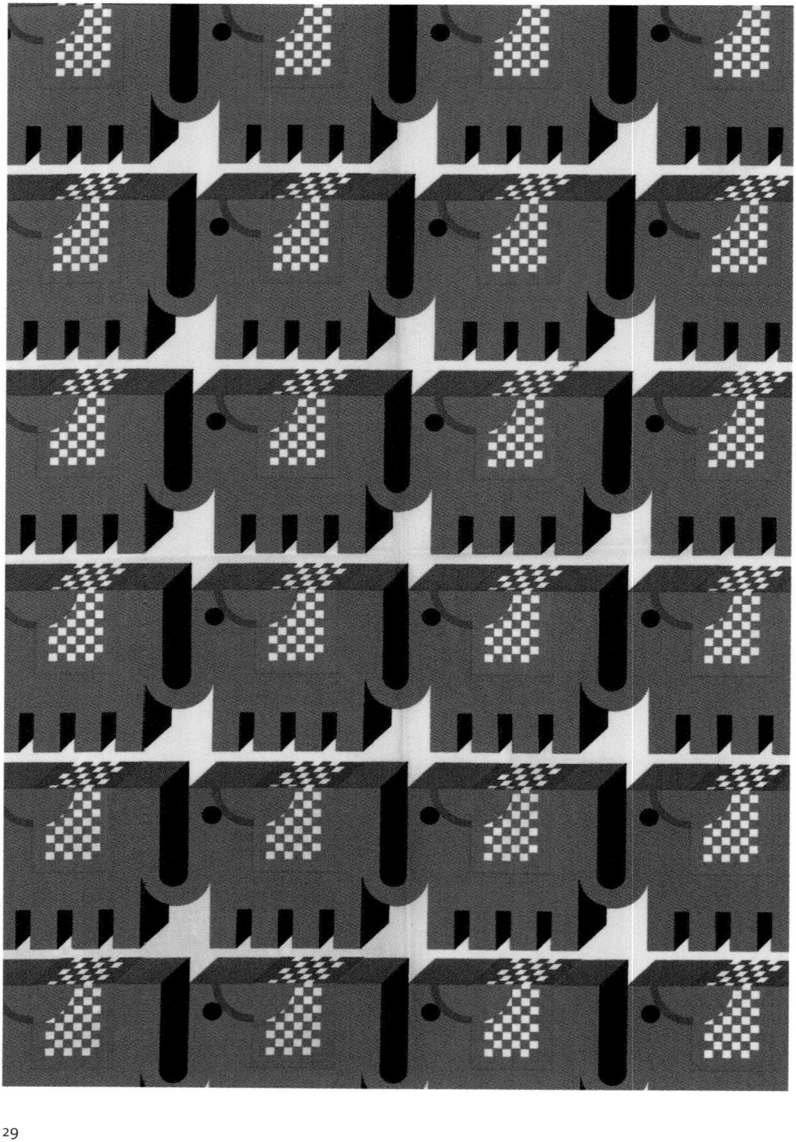

29
Neil Bradburn/Heal's
Small Elephants, furnishing fabric (see also plate 30). Printed cotton. UK, 1974 (V&A: T.268:2–1999)

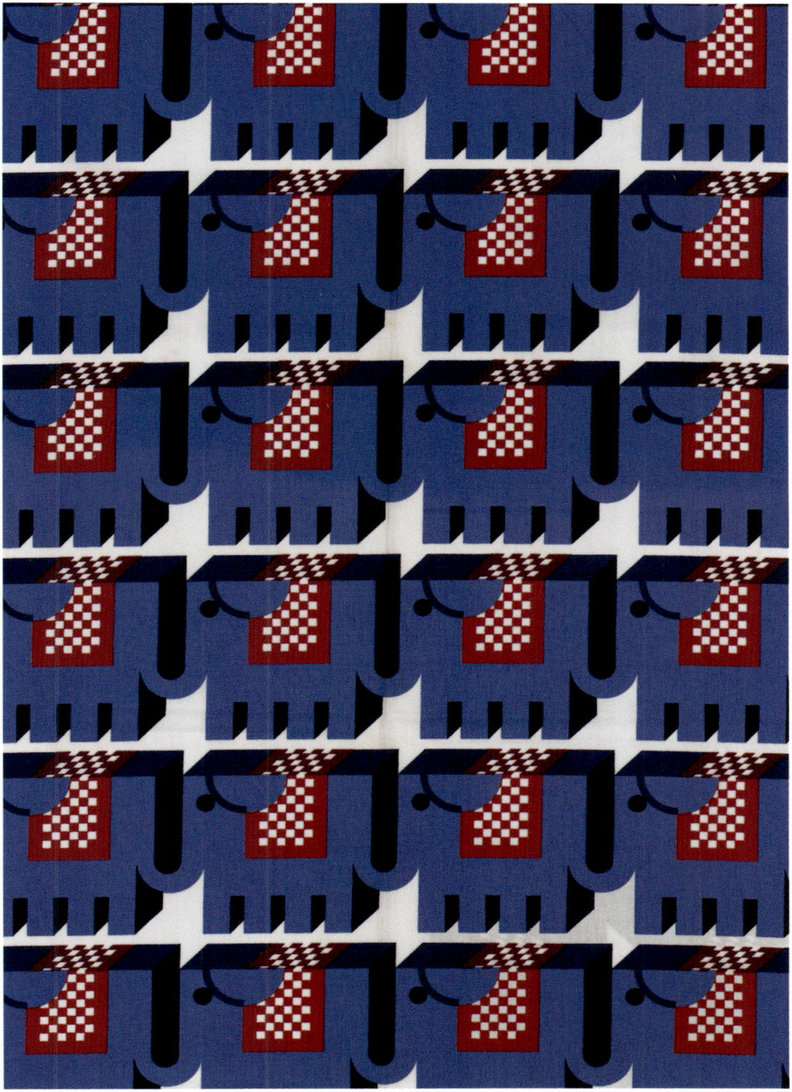

30
Neil Bradburn/Heal's
Small Elephants, furnishing fabric (see also plate 29). Printed cotton. UK, 1974 (V&A: T.268:1–1999)

31
Tony Fraser/Arthur Sanderson & Sons Ltd
Neon, wallpaper (see also plate 32). Screen-printed paper. UK, 1971 (V&A: E.231–1977)

32
Tony Fraser/Arthur Sanderson & Sons Ltd
Neon, wallpaper (see also plate 31). Screen-printed paper. UK, 1971 (V&A: E.232–1977)

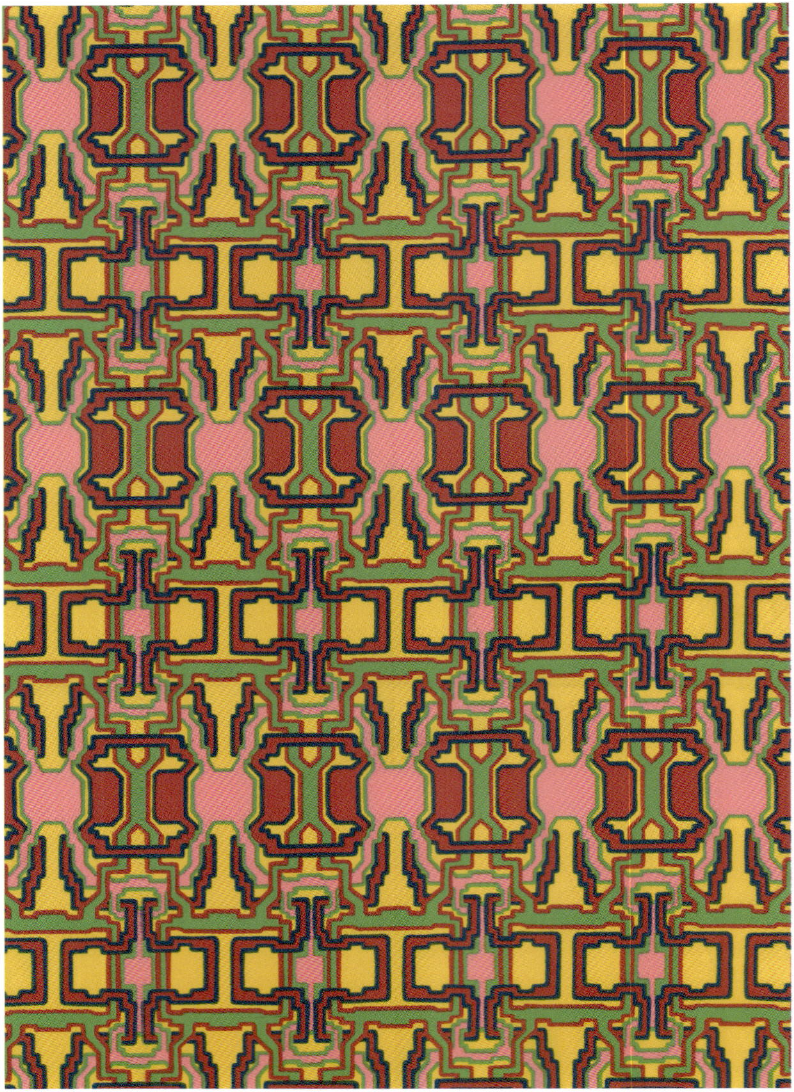

33
Edward Squires/ Warner and Sons Ltd
Colourtron, furnishing fabric. Printed cotton. UK, 1968 (V&A: Circ.801–1968)

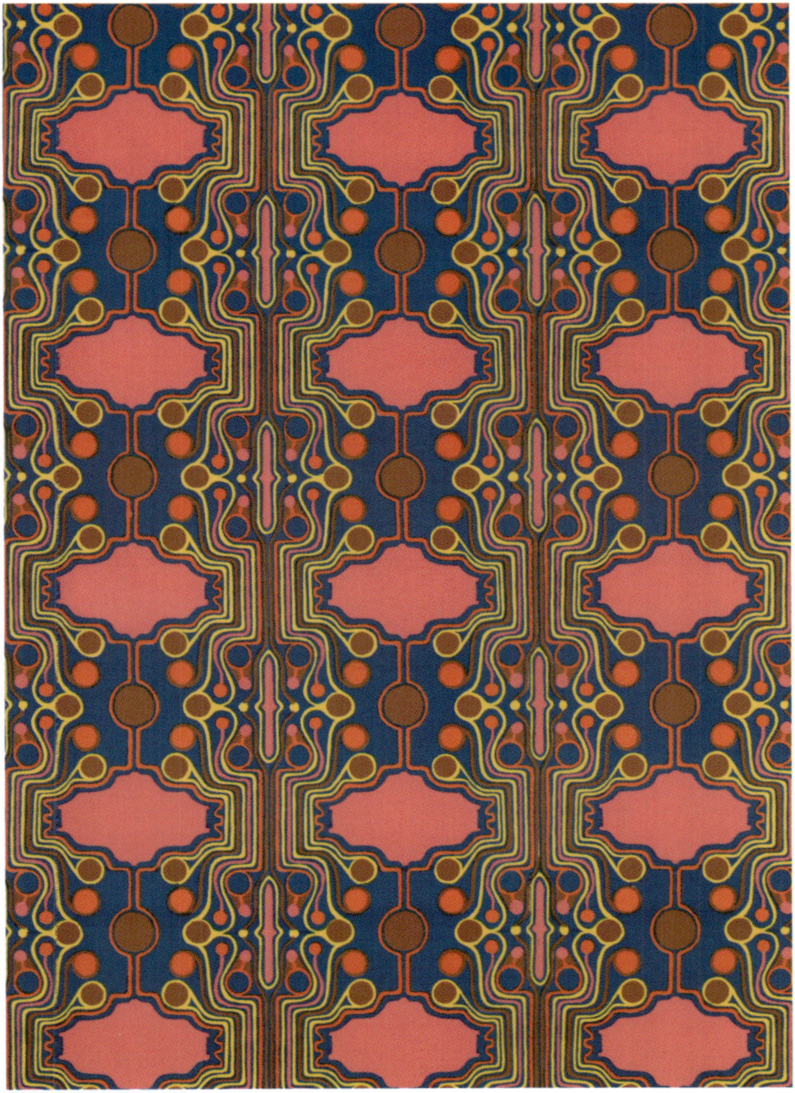

34
Edward Squires/Warner and Sons Ltd
Circuit, furnishing fabric. Printed cotton. UK, 1968 (V&A: Circ.802–1968)

35
Edward Squires/Warner and Sons Ltd
Lunar Rocket, furnishing fabric. Screen-printed cotton. UK, 1969 (V&A: Circ.45A–1970)

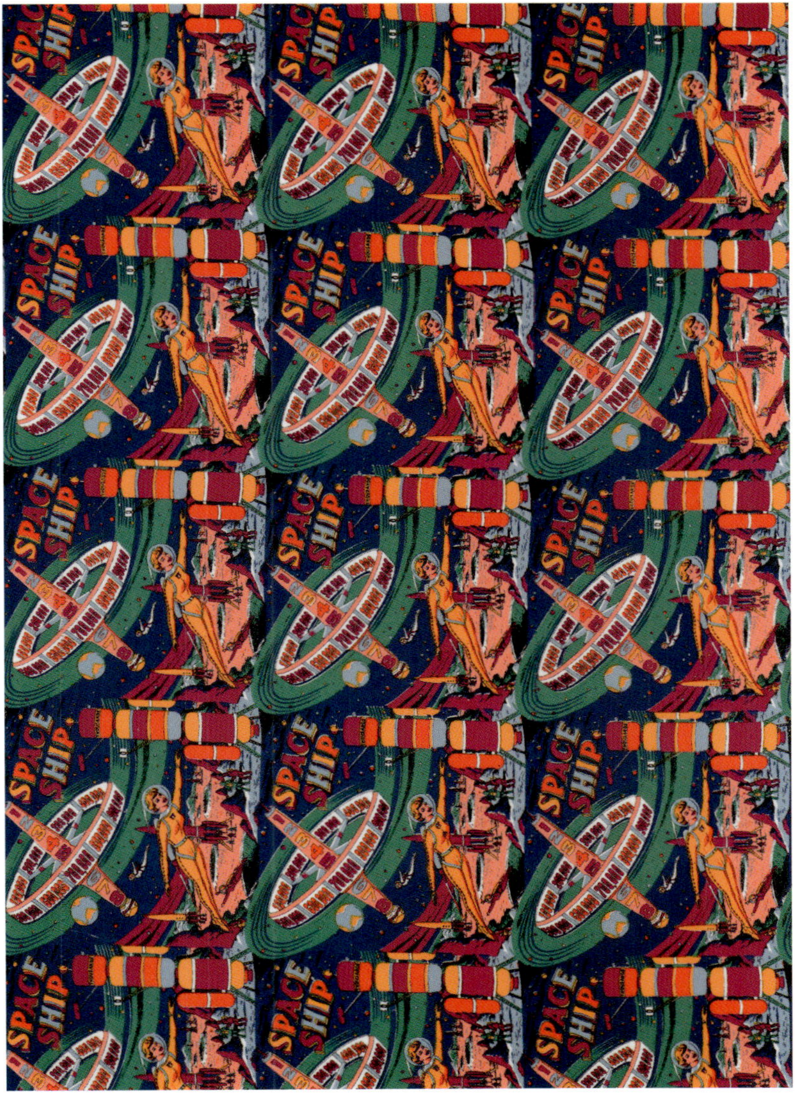

36
Stephanie Huber/Ferrer y Sentis
Space Ship, dress fabric. Printed synthetic jersey. Spain, 1973 (V&A: Circ.299–1973)

37
Sue Palmer/Warner and Sons
Space Walk, furnishing fabric. Printed cotton. UK, 1970 (V&A: Circ.44–1970)

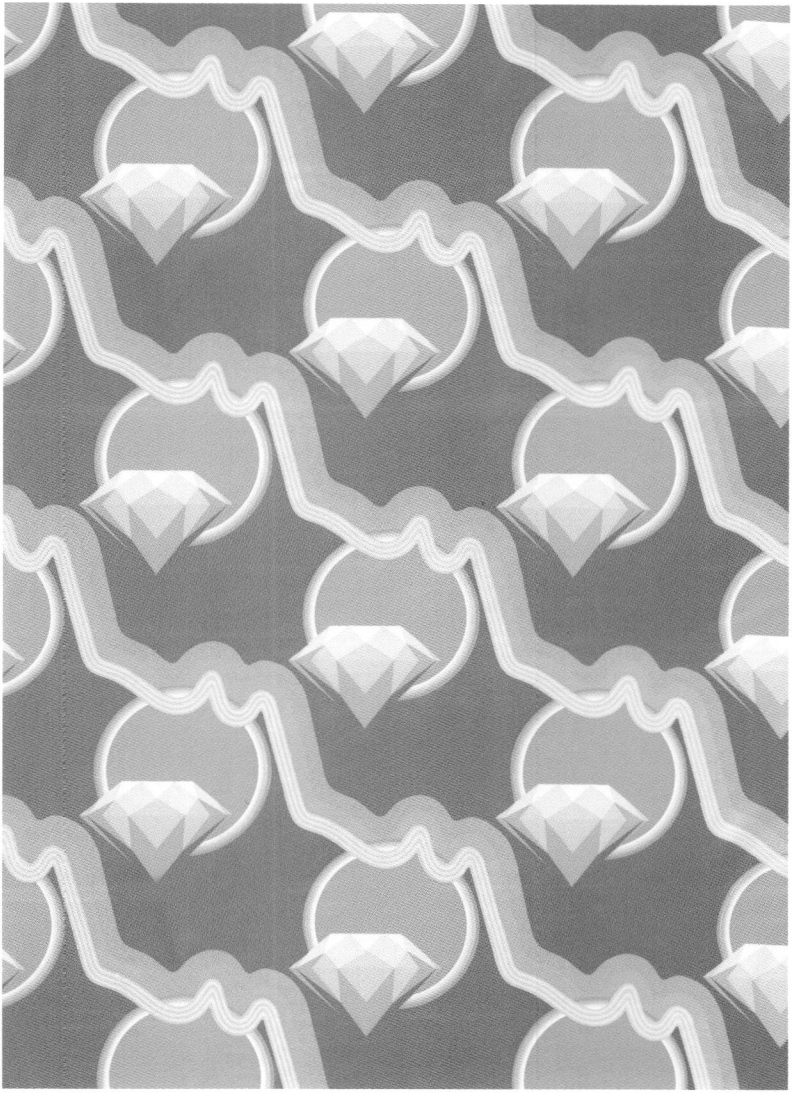

38
Sue Palmer/Warner and Sons
Jewelled Sky, furnishing fabric. Printed cotton. UK, 1972 (V&A: Circ.334–1972)

39
Zandra Rhodes/Heal's
Gala, furnishing fabric. Printed cotton. UK, 1964 (V&A: Circ.746–1964)

40
Shirley Craven/Hull Traders Ltd
Five, furnishing fabric. Screen-printed cotton. UK, 1966 (V&A: Circ.760–1967)

41
Fieldcrest Inc.
Funny Sheets, furnishing fabric. Roller-printed cotton. USA, 1972 (V&A: Circ.228–1972)

42
Leon Rosenblatt/Concord Fabrics Inc.
Love Comic, dress fabric. Roller-printed cotton. USA, 1970 (V&A: Circ.193–1974)

43
Marshall Lester/Scott Lester Ltd
Liberty Belle, T-shirt. Roller-printed cotton knit. UK, 1973–4 (V&A: Circ.445–1974)

44
Marshall Lester/Scott Lester Ltd
Ship Mates, T-shirt. Roller-printed cotton knit. UK, 1973–4 (V&A: Circ.444–1974)

45
Marshall Lester/Scott Lester Ltd
Cycling, T-shirt. Roller-printed cotton knit. UK, 1973–4 (V&A: Circ.448–1974)

46
Marshall Lester/Scott Lester Ltd
Football, T-shirt. Roller-printed cotton knit. UK, 1973–4 (V&A: Circ.447–1974)

47
Stephanie Huber/Ferrer y Sentis
Monte Carlo, dress fabric. Printed synthetic jersey. Spain, 1973 (V&A: Circ.300–1973)

48
Mr Freedom
Man's shirt. Printed nylon. UK, 1971 (V&A: T.209–1974)

49
Stephanie Huber/Ferrer y Sentis
Derby, dress fabric. Printed synthetic jersey. Spain, 1973 (V&A: Circ.298–1973)

50
Stephanie Huber/Ferrer y Sentis
Rainbow, dress fabric. Printed synthetic jersey. Spain, 1973 (V&A: Circ.301–1973)

51
Stephanie Huber/Ferrer y Sentis
Hootenanny, dress fabric. Printed synthetic jersey. Spain, 1973 (V&A: Circ.297–1973)

52
John Dove/Wonder Workshop
Western Movies, furnishing fabric. Photo-printed cotton calico. UK, 1974 (V&A: Circ.441–1974)

53
Christopher Snow/Slick Brands
Chuck Berry, dress fabric. Screen-printed satin. UK, 1974 (V&A: Circ.443–1974)

54
Christopher Snow/Slick Brands
Marilyn, dress fabric. Screen-printed crêpe. UK, 1974 (V&A: Circ.450–1974)

55
Mary Oliver/Heal's
Kew, furnishing fabric. Printed cotton. UK, 1974 (V&A: Circ.182–1974)

56
In Fabrics Ltd
Flowers, furnishing fabric. Roller-printed cotton. USA, 1973 (V&A: Circ.303–1974)

57
Avondale Mills Inc.
Faces, furnishing fabric. Screen-printed cotton. USA, 1971 (V&A: Circ.16–1972)

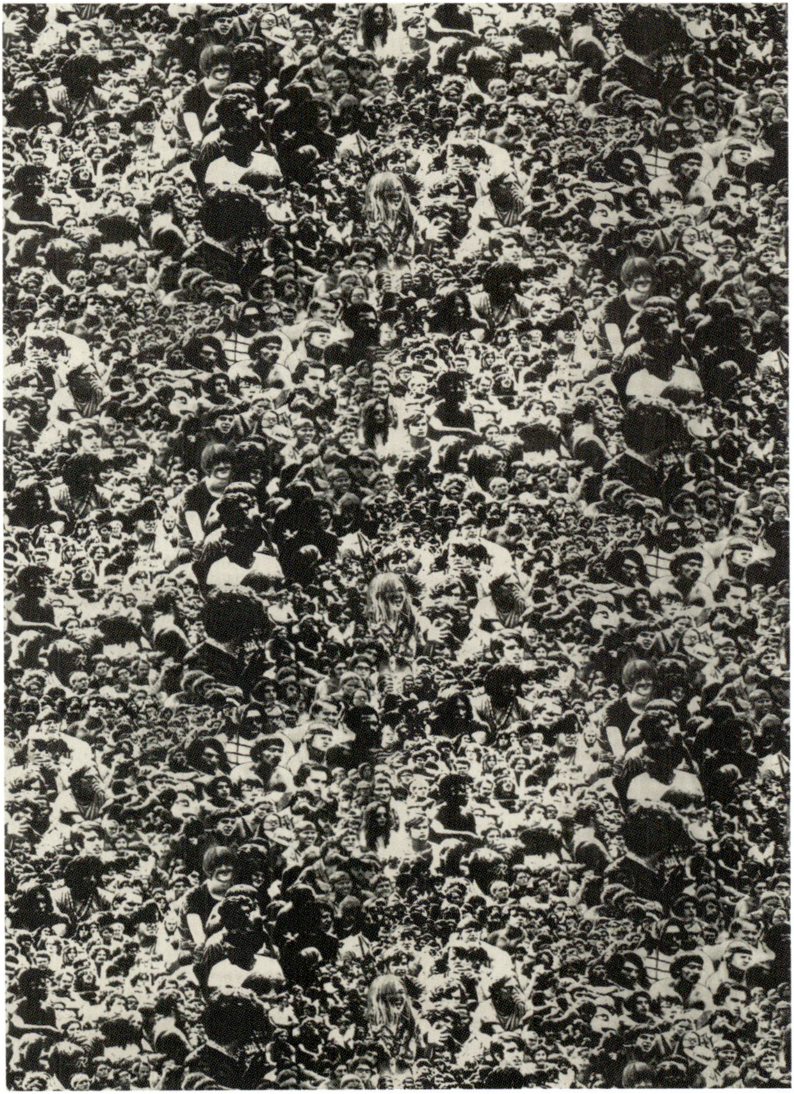

58
Avondale Mills Inc.
Woodstock, furnishing fabric. Screen-printed cotton. USA, 1971 (V&A: Circ.21–1972)

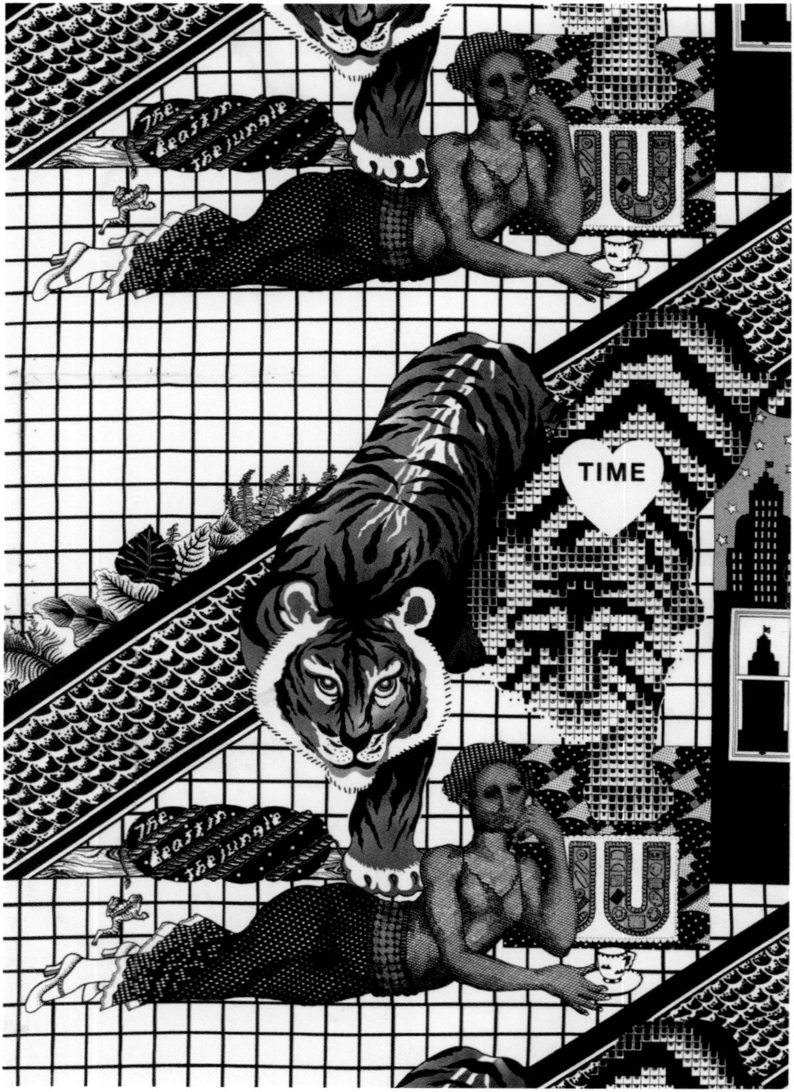

59
Francis Butler/Goodstuffs Inc.
Beast in the Jungle, furnishing fabric. Screen-printed cotton. USA, 1973 (V&A: Circ.7–1974)

60
J & M Dove/Wonder Workshop
Wild Thing, dress fabric. Screen-printed cotton jersey. UK, 1972 (V&A: Circ.3–1974)

61
J & M Dove/Wonder Workshop
Elvis, dress fabric. Screen-printed cotton jersey. UK, 1971 (V&A: Circ.2–1974)

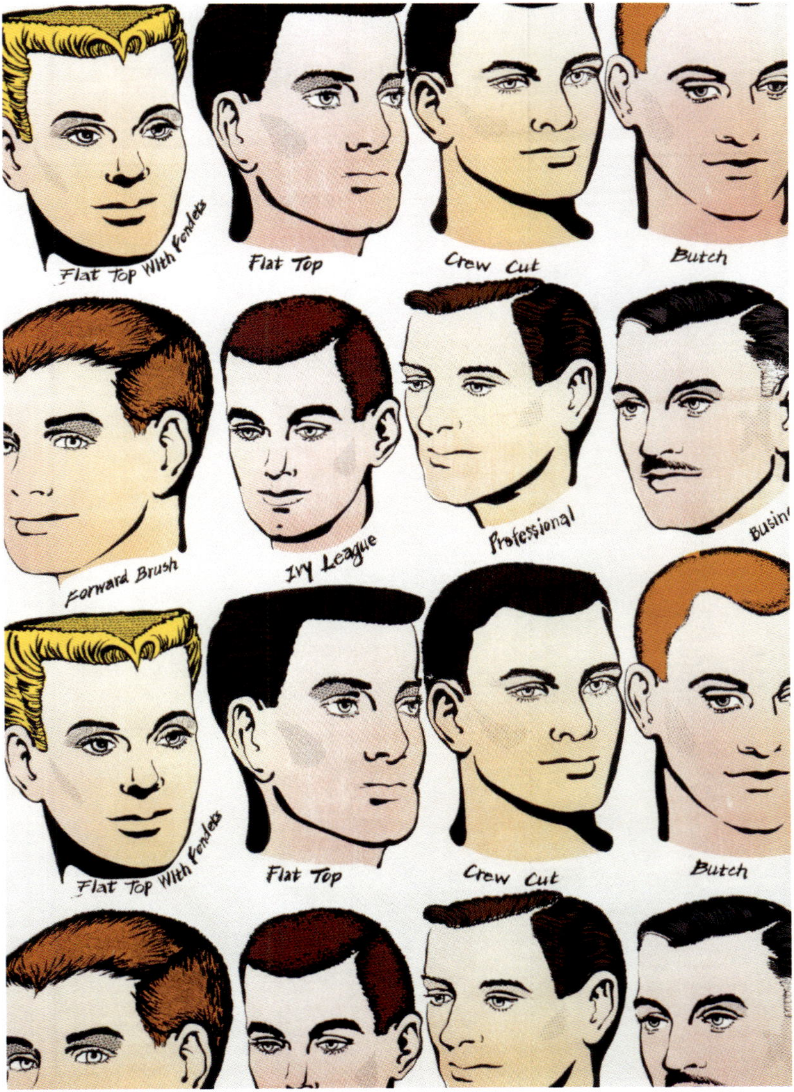

62
Marc Foster Grant/Michael Yates
Haircut? Yes, Please!, furnishing fabric. Screen-printed satin. UK, 1973 (V&A: Circ.189–1974)

63
Lloyd Johnson/Patrick Lloyd
Fred, furnishing fabric. Screen-printed silk. UK, 1973 (V&A: Circ.303–1973)

64
Jane Wealleans/OK Textiles Ltd
Legs, furnishing fabric. Screen-printed silk. UK, 1973 (V&A: Circ.169–1973)

65
Hayes Textiles Ltd
Fairytale Castles, head tie. Jacquard woven silk. Switzerland, 1982–3 (V&A: T.129:1–2000)

66
Hayes Textiles Ltd
Guardsman, head tie. Jacquard woven silk. Switzerland, 1980s (V&A: T.124–2000)

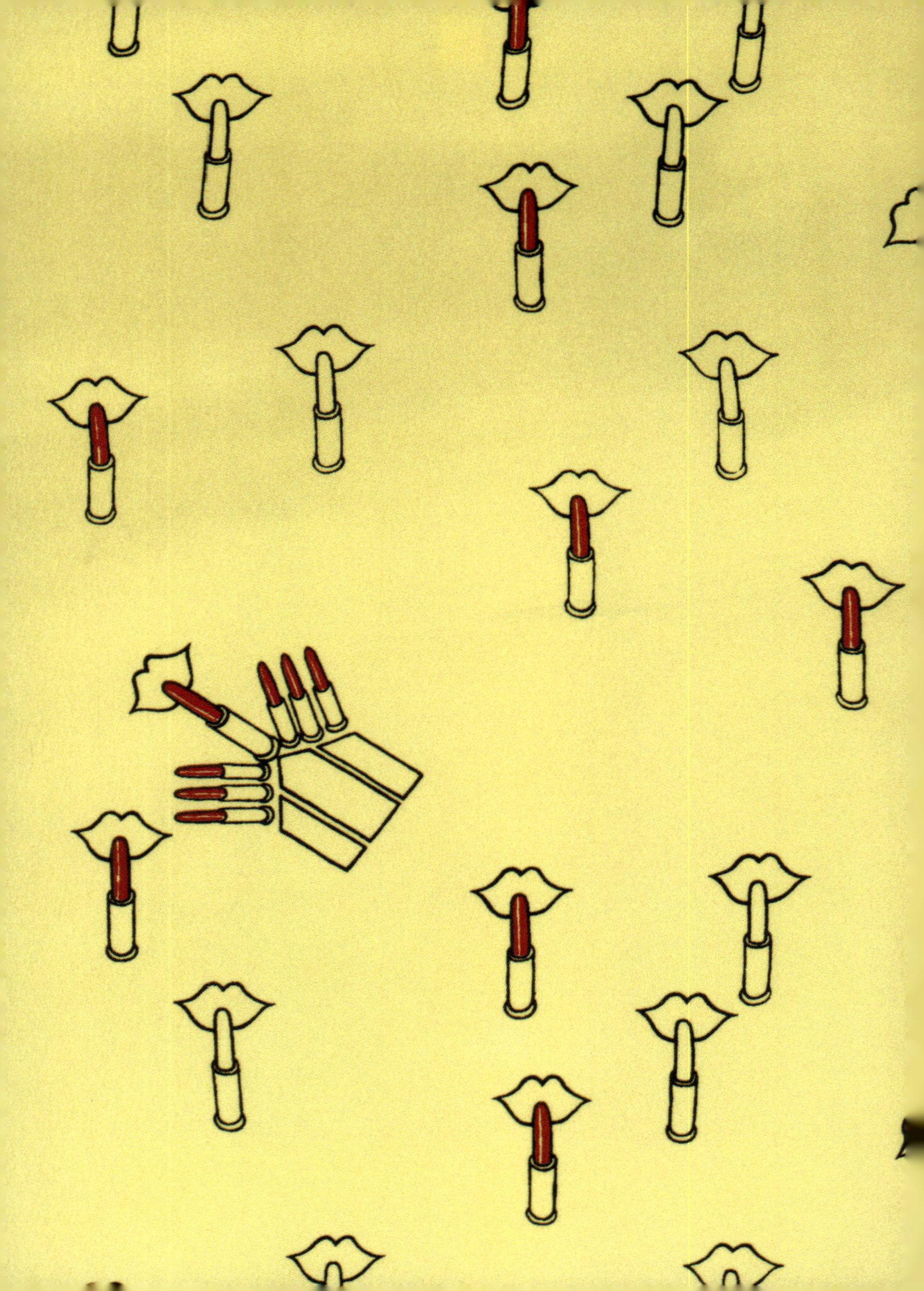

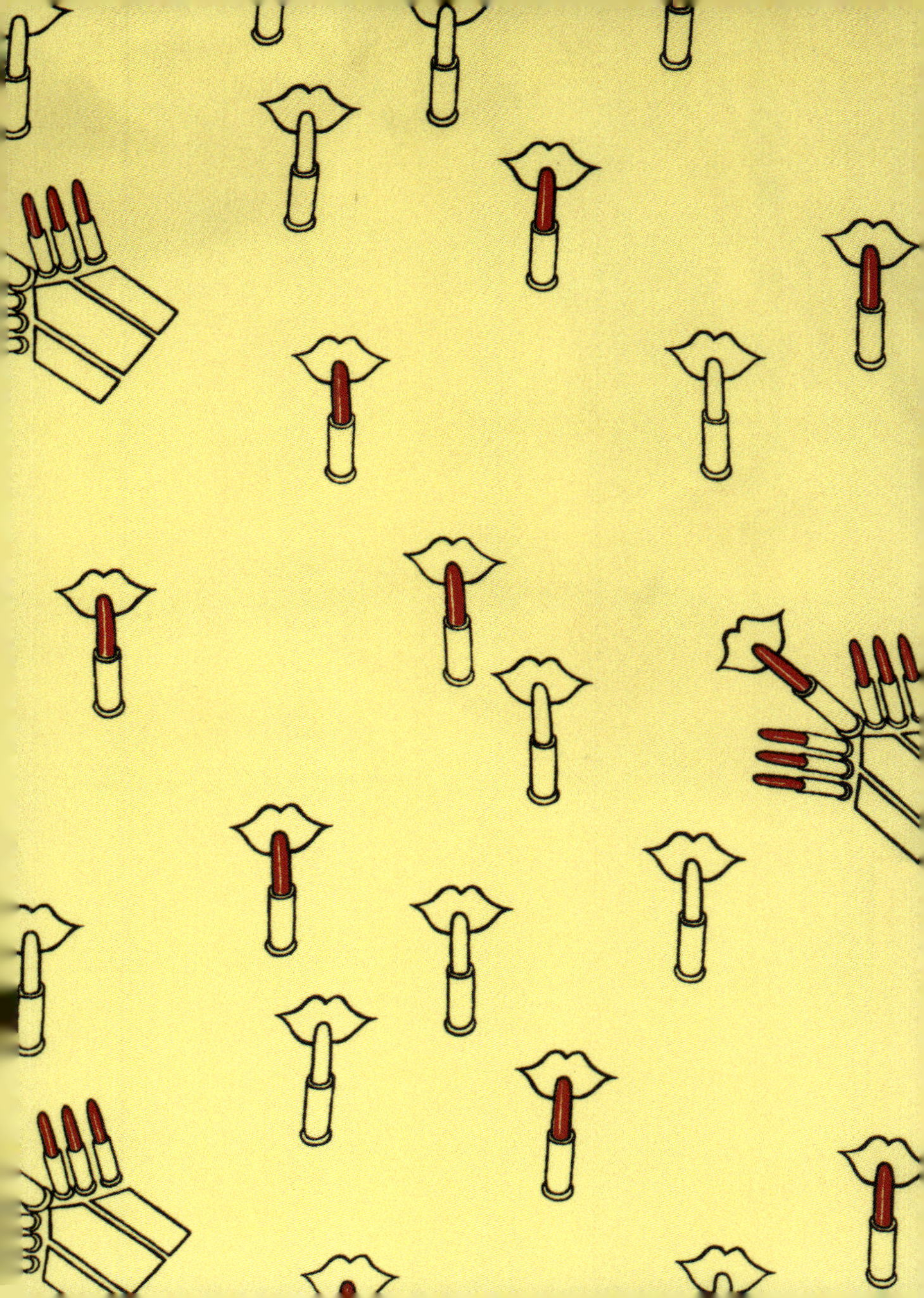

Further Reading

Fogg, Marnie
1960s Fashion Print: A Sourcebook
Batsford, 2008

Jackson, Lesley
Twentieth-Century Pattern Design
New York, 2007

Jackson, Lesley
The Sixties
London, 2000

Korosec, Constance and Pina, Leslie A.
Fashion Fabrics: 1960s
Pennsylvania, 1998

Nakayama, Masanari
Pop & Modern
Tokyo, 2007

Digital Images

The patterns reproduced in this book are stored on the accompanying compact disc as jpeg files (at approximately A5-size, 300 dpi). You should be able to open them, and manipulate them, direct from the CD-ROM in most modern image software (on Windows or Mac platforms), and no installation should be required (although we, as publishers, cannot guarantee absolutely that the disk will be accessible for every computer).

Instructions for tracing and tiling the images will be found with the documentation for your software.

The names of the files correspond to the V&A inventory numbers of the images.